COUNTRIES OF THE WORLD

INDIA

Columbia City, IN

MICHAEL ALLABY

Facts On File, Inc.

TITLES IN THE COUNTRIES OF THE WORLD SERIES:
ARGENTINA • AUSTRALIA • BRAZIL • CANADA • CHINA EGYPT • FRANCE • GERMANY • INDIA • ITALY • JAPAN KENYA • MEXICO • NIGERIA • POLAND • UNITED KINGDOM UNITED STATES • VIETNAM

India

Copyright © 2005 by Evans Brothers, Limited

All rights reserved. No part of this book may be reproduced or utilized in any form or by any means, electronic or mechanical, including photocopying, recording, or by any information storage or retrieval systems, without permission in writing from the publisher. For information contact:

Facts On File, Inc.
132 West 31st Street
New York NY 10001

Library of Congress Cataloging-in-Publication Data

Allaby, Michael
   India/Michael Allaby.
      p.cm. — (Countries of the world)
   Includes index.
   ISBN 0-8160-6006-1
      1. India. I. Title. II. Countries of the world (Facts On File, Inc.)

   DS407.A595 2005
   954—dc22   2005040683

Facts On File books are available at special discounts when purchased in bulk quantities for businesses, associations, institutions, or sales promotions. Please call our Special Sales Department in New York at (212) 967-8800 or (800) 322-8755.

You can find Facts On File on the World Wide Web at http://www.factsonfile.com.

Printed in China by Leo Paper Products, Ltd.

10 9 8 7 6 5 4 3 2 1

Editor: Daniel Rogers
Designer: Victoria Webb
Picture researchers: Lynda Lines and Frances Bailey
Map artwork: Peter Bull
Charts and graphs: Encompass Graphics, Ltd.

First published by Evans Brothers Limited, 2A Portman Mansions, Chiltern Street, London W1U 6NR, United Kingdom

This edition published under license from Evans Brothers Limited. All rights reserved.

Photograph acknowledgments
All by Mark Henley except: front cover upper middle, 27, 56 top (MPM Images); front cover lower middle, 6–7, 10 top, 44 both, 61 (Thirdangle.com); front endpapers, 57 (Corbis Digital Stock); 8, 46 (Hartmut Schwarzbach, Still Pictures); 9, 52 bottom (Anders Gunnartz, Still Pictures); 10 bottom (David Samuel Robbins, Corbis); 12, 16 top (Lindsay Hebberd, Corbis); 13 top (Kamal Kishore, Reuters); 13 bottom (David Brinicombe, Eye Ubiquitous/Hutchison); 14, 48 right, 56 bottom (Shehzad Noorani, Still Pictures); 15 top, 31 top, 33 top, 42, 43, 45, 54 bottom (Mark Edwards, Still Pictures); 16 bottom (Chris Lisle, Corbis); 17 (DPL/Link India, Link Picture Library); 18 (Mary Jelliffe, Eye Ubiquitous/Hutchison); 19 (Nick Haslam, Eye Ubiquitous/Hutchison); 21, 22, 51 bottom (Sherwin Crasto, Reuters); 22–23 (Utpal Barvah, Reuters); 23, 33 bottom (Joerg Boethling, Still Pictures); 26 bottom (Wolfgang Schmidt, Still Pictures); 29 top (Patricio Goycoolea, Eye Ubiquitous/Hutchison); 29 bottom (S. Ganguly/UNEP, Still Pictures); 31 bottom (Ron Giling, Still Pictures); 34 bottom, 39 bottom (Pawel Kopczynski, Reuters); 35 (Singh/UNEP, Still Pictures); 36 top (Johann Scheibner, Still Pictures); 36 bottom (Sebastian Bolesch, Still Pictures); 37 (Jayanta Shaw, Reuters); 38 (Karamallah Daher, Reuters); 41 (Bennett Dean, Eye Ubiquitous/Hutchison); 47 (Hoescht Marion Roussel, Still Pictures); 49 (Chris Martin, Still Pictures); 50 (SIPA, Rex Features); 52 top (Indranil Mukherjee, Getty Images); 55 (Fateh Singh Rathore, Still Pictures).

Endpapers (front): The Taj Mahal at Agra, Uttar Pradesh, perhaps the world's most famous building.
Title page: A farmer in Orissa using oxen to plow his paddy field.
Imprint and Contents pages: Pushkar Lake, Rajasthan, with the city behind. Pushkar is a place of pilgrimage for Hindus.
Endpapers (back): A view of Mumbai from the sea.

The Indian flag consists of three bands: orange representing courage and sacrifice, white for purity and green for growth. The central wheel symbol, or chakra, signifies that in life there is movement.

Morning at Varanasi, when Hindus ritually bathe in the Ganges River.

India is the world's seventh-largest country and has the second-largest population. Its civilization is one of the world's oldest and richest, stretching back for more than 4,000 years to a sophisticated culture that flourished in the Indus Valley. Today India combines ancient traditions with modern industries and scientific institutions.

STATES AND TERRITORIES OF INDIA

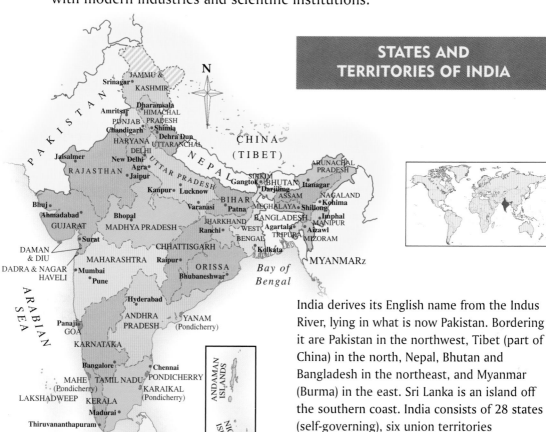

India derives its English name from the Indus River, lying in what is now Pakistan. Bordering it are Pakistan in the northwest, Tibet (part of China) in the north, Nepal, Bhutan and Bangladesh in the northeast, and Myanmar (Burma) in the east. Sri Lanka is an island off the southern coast. India consists of 28 states (self-governing), six union territories (administered by the central government) and the national capital territory of New Delhi.

New Delhi, the Indian capital city, seen from the air.

MANY LANGUAGES, MANY RELIGIONS

India's people and cultures are as diverse as its landscapes. Hindi and English are the official languages, but these are two among many. Hindi, with its associated dialects, is the native language of less than half the population, and English is not an Indian language at all. Two thirds of the population understand Hindi and less than one fifth understand English.

Hinduism is the religion of almost three quarters of the population. Every town has fine temples, and Hindu festivals are colorful, often involving processions of elaborately costumed figures. About 12 percent of the population are Muslims and there are also Christians, Sikhs and Buddhists.

In contrast with the ornate architecture and spectacle, however, there are also areas of desperate poverty and severe deprivation. As the Indian economy continues to grow, little by little that poverty will diminish.

CONTRASTING LANDSCAPES

India is a land of many landscapes. The mighty Himalayan range in the north contains several of the world's highest mountains. It is a region of snow, cold winds and bare rock. In the northwest, the Thar or Great Indian Desert is a dry, inhospitable place, but on the other side of the country, in the northeast, there are tropical rain forests. There are also mangrove forests, swamps and vast expanses of rich farmland.

Together, India, Pakistan and Bangladesh are often called the Indian Subcontinent. The name is doubly appropriate: Geographic barriers separate this region from the main part of Asia, making it distinct, and it is also geologically distinct. India was not always attached to Asia. It was once a separate landmass, which drifted northward and collided with southern Asia about 40 million years ago. It was that collision which raised the Himalayas, and India is still thrusting into Asia, so the mountains are still rising.

KEY DATA	
Official Name:	Bharat (Hindi) Republic of India (English)
Area:	3,166,414km²
Population:	1,027,015,247 (2001)
Official Languages:	Hindi, English
Main Cities:	New Delhi (capital), Mumbai, Kolkata, Bangalore, Chennai, Ahmadabad, Pune, Hyderabad, Kanpur, Surat, Jaipur
GDP Per Capita:	US$ 2,670*
Currency:	Indian rupee (Re; plural Rs); 1 Re = 100 paise
Exchange Rate:	1 US$ = Rs 43.77 1 UK£ = Rs 82.46

*(2002) Calculated on Purchasing Power Parity basis. Sources: *CIA World Factbook, 2004*; World Bank; UN Human Development Report, 2003

The Himalayan ranges, seen from the city of Shimla, Himachal Pradesh. The world's highest mountains are in the most distant range.

The Earth's outermost solid layer, or crust, consists of rigid sections, or plates, that move in relation to one another. India sits on the Indian Plate, which also includes the floor of part of the surrounding Arabian Sea and Indian Ocean. Geologically, India is distinct from Asia. That fact and the consequences of the collision between the Indian and Eurasian Plates give India its physical structure and landscape and account for the contrast between northern and southern India.

THE NORTHERN MOUNTAINS

About 200 million years ago, all the continents were joined together into a single supercontinent called Pangaea. Soon after that the supercontinent began to break up, and that is when India separated from its neighbors and began its slow northward drift from deep in the Southern Hemisphere. It crossed the equator about 60 million years ago, and 40 million years ago the Indian Plate collided with the southern margin of the Eurasian Plate. That collision crumpled the rocks to the north, raising the Tibetan Plateau and the Himalaya Mountains. The mountains form the first of India's landscapes, and a barrier separating India from Central Asia.

A mountain road in Himachal Pradesh.

The northernmost range is the Great Himalayas, where the average elevation is 6,000m. The Great Himalayas include all of the highest mountains. In the west, where India, Pakistan and China meet, this range merges with the Karakoram Range.

To the south of the Great Himalayas are the Lesser Himalayas. Mountains in this range are between 1,500m and 5,000m high. The Lesser Himalayas extend across northern India, through the states of Himachal Pradesh, Uttar Pradesh, Sikkim and Arunachal Pradesh. The cities of Shimla and Darjiling (or Darjeeling), where the British once took shelter from the intense summer heat, are located in the Lesser Himalayas.

The Southern or Outer Himalayas are the most southerly of the three ranges. These mountains are the Himalayan foothills, averaging 900–1,200m high. In Himachal Pradesh and Uttar Pradesh this range is known as the Siwalik Hills.

Shimla, Himachal Pradesh, is where Europeans formerly retreated during the hottest part of the year. Many of the buildings look British.

THE HIMALAYAN REGION AND THE FOOTHILLS

The Himalayas are the highest mountains in the world. Everest, the tallest mountain, rising to 8,850m, lies on the border between Nepal and China. K2 is 8,611m tall and lies in a region claimed by India, Pakistan and China. Kanchenjunga, on the India-Nepal border, is 8,586m high, and the peak of Nanda Devi, in India, is 7,817m.

Permanent snow covers the Himalayas above 4,500–6,000m on the southern slopes and above 5,500–6,000m on the northern side. Below the snow line, the northern slopes are mainly forested, but the southern slopes are bare.

There is not one Himalayan range, however, but three parallel ranges. Together they are about 2,400km long and 240–330km wide.

Terraces of rice fields in Kullu Valley, Himachal Pradesh.

MOUNTAIN VALLEYS

Between the ranges there are high plateaus and fertile valleys, as well as deep gorges cut by the rivers that cascade down the mountainsides. The Kullu Valley in Himachal Pradesh is one of the most beautiful of the Himalayan valleys, stretching southward for 80km on either side of the Beas River, with apple orchards, meadows and rice fields set against the mountain backdrop. The valley has been inhabited for thousands of years. Kulantapith, its ancient Sanskrit name, means "end of the habitable world."

THE INDO-GANGETIC PLAIN

At the southern foot of the Himalayas there is a deep depression where the solid rocks lie below sea level. Over millions of years, this depression has filled with soil washed down from the mountains. Today this region

CASE STUDY
THE INDUS VALLEY CIVILIZATION

Patna, then called Pataliputra, was founded in 600 B.C., and in 321 B.C. Chandragupta, who established the first Indian empire, made it his capital. He then expanded his empire westward all the way to the Indus. The Indo-Gangetic Plain is the region where Indian civilization began, although it started long before the reign of Chandragupta. From about 2500 B.C., farms in the Indus Valley were raising livestock and growing grains, dates, melons and possibly cotton. They sent their produce to several large cities, including Mohenjo Daro, Harappa, Lothal and Dholavira. Lothal was an important port, trading with Persia and Mesopotamia. The Indus Valley civilization disappeared around 1700 B.C., probably because the climate became much drier and the crops failed.

includes the floodplains of the Indus and Ganges Rivers. In the west the mighty Indus, with its tributaries, crosses the plains of Punjab and Haryana. The rivers Jhelum, Chenab, Ravi, Beas and Sutlej surround the Punjab plain; the name *Punjab* is derived from the Persian *panj ab,* meaning "five rivers." The Ganges or Ganga rises in an ice cave at the foot of the Gangotri Glacier in the Himalayas. The river then passes through the mountains of Uttaranchal and crosses the plains of Uttar Pradesh, Bihar and West Bengal, ending in a vast delta in Bangladesh known as the Padma that merges with the Bay of Bengal.

RICH LAND

The Indo-Gangetic Plain, comprising the land of the Indus and Ganges river systems, has rich soil watered by seasonal rains and irrigation channels from the rivers. The plain is the agricultural heartland of India. More than half

Farmworkers harvesting wheat by hand in a field on the outskirts of New Delhi. Harvesting this way is slow and very hard work.

of India's rice, wheat and millet are grown in Punjab and Haryana. Patna, the capital city of Bihar and one of the oldest cities in India, gives its name to a variety of long-grained rice that is very popular in the West.

A pilgrim bathing at the source of the Ganges, high in the mountains.

THE SUNDARBANS

Kolkata (formerly called Calcutta) lies on the Hooghly (or Hugli) River, the westernmost branch of the Ganges, which divides into many streams as it enters the lower Gangetic Plain in West Bengal. To the south of the city, the Hooghly and Ganges Delta forms an expanse of marshland, mangrove forest, and small islands covering 10,000km². This region is known as the Sundarbans, or "beautiful forest," and is one of the most famous features of eastern India. Large parts of the area are protected as nature reserves.

The Sundarbans teems with wildlife. There are saltwater crocodiles, Ganges dolphins, sea turtles, and sharks, as well as spotted deer and wild boar. The most famous residents, however, are the Bengal tigers. Tigers swim well and can move freely among the islands.

Woodcutters, fisherfolk and honey collectors also live in the Sunderbans. All of them respect and worship Banbibi, goddess of the beautiful forest, and her husband Dakshin Rai, the supreme ruler of the Sunderbans.

THE DECCAN

The Vindhya and Satpura Ranges of hills and the Chota Nagpur Plateau in southern Bihar separate the northern regions of India from the Indian Peninsula. The interior of the peninsula comprises a series of plateaus averaging 300–750m above sea level and intersected by rivers flowing eastward into the Bay of Bengal. This region of rolling hills is known as the Deccan.

The Deccan is tilted, with the land higher in the west than in the east. It is bordered

Members of the Mowali tribe, gathering honey in the Sunderbans mangrove forest.

by hills, called the Western and Eastern Ghats, which meet at the tip of the peninsula. Coastal plains surround the Deccan. The western plains contain tidal salt marshes, lagoons and fine, sandy beaches. On the eastern side the plain is wider and very fertile.

The Deccan lies at the geographic and cultural heart of India. The Vindhya and Satpura hills are in Madhya Pradesh State, which stretches across the center of the country. Its hills are covered with scrub vegetation and during the dry season its plains are scorched by the fierce sun, but it also contains Bandhavgarh and Kanha National Parks, with tigers, mongooses and eagles. Rudyard Kipling's *Jungle Book* stories are set in Kanha National Park. Bhopal, the state capital, is a vibrant, fast-growing city.

On its southeastern side, Madhya Pradesh adjoins Chhattisgarh, a state founded in November 2000. Chhattisgarh contains one third of India's forests. Many of its people practice a traditional, tribal way of life.

ABOVE: A view across the Deccan, which covers much of the interior of India.

BELOW: A small boat carrying passengers and their bicycles passes palm trees lining one of the many waterways in Kerala.

The Kailasanatha Temple at Ellora, Maharashtra, was carved out of the rock face in the eighth century.

SOUTHERN INDIA

Maharashtra lies to the south of Madhya Pradesh, and its capital is Mumbai (formerly Bombay). It is highly industrialized, but as well as the petrochemical works and factories, in the hills there are farming villages and market towns. The hills of the Western Ghats are green, and farms on the inland plateau grow cotton and fruits, including oranges, sapodilla and mangoes.

Andhra Pradesh is the largest Indian state. There are beaches along the northern part of the coast, and farther south the coastal plain is an important rice-growing area. Inland, the plateau is rocky. Hyderabad, the state capital, was founded in 1591 and built on a grid pattern, with streets crossing at right angles. It was once home to wealthy rulers called nizams, who controlled Hyderabad from Golconda, a fortified city covering 40km^2, with palaces, mosques, and gardens on a hill overlooking the city. There were diamond mines nearby, from which came the Kohinoor diamond, the world's most famous jewel,

which is now part of the British crown jewels. The palaces of the nizams still survive as museums. Outside the museums there are countless bazaars. Today the city has a high-tech industrial district, called Cyberabad. To the north, a twin city, Secunderabad, has absorbed the expansion of Hyderabad.

A young woman collecting ripe coffee berries on a plantation in Karnataka.

To the west of Andhra Pradesh, Karnataka extends to the Western Ghats, where coffee, fruits and spices grow on the fertile hillsides. Tamil Nadu, the southernmost state, is a land of paddy fields and palm forests.

Orissa occupies the thickly wooded Eastern Ghats and the lush, fertile coastal plain. Inland is the Simplipal National Park, with tigers, elephants, and many other animals.

In the far west, a region of desert and marshland called Kutch (or Kachchh) is home to seminomadic pastoral communities renowned for their craft products (see below). India and Pakistan fought for Kutch. In 1968 the United Nations (UN) resolved the matter and Kutch became part of India. In 2001 an earthquake caused widespread devastation around the main city of Bhuj.

CASE STUDY
PASTORALISTS OF KUTCH

Kutch is in northwestern Gujarat, bordering Pakistan in the far northwest of India. Northern Kutch has too dry a climate for growing crops. There is pasture for livestock, however, and the people are pastoralists. They live by tending herds of camels, cattle, buffalo, goats and sheep. The animals graze the pasture, and when there is no more food the herders move them to the next area. Herders and livestock follow regular routes from pasture to pasture to take advantage of the seasonal rains, remaining for only a short time at each site. Pastoral people live a seminomadic life.

Nomads live in dwellings that can be taken down and carried from place to place. Seminomads have more permanent homes. While the men are away tending the livestock, the women, children and old people of Kutch stay at home making the craft goods that are an important source of income.

A goatherd with his animals in the Rann of Kutch, Gujarat.

A village near Jaisalmer in the Thar Desert. The dwellings are made from mud with thatched roofs.

Cape Comorin, at the southern tip of India, is at 8° north latitude. The northernmost part of India is at 35° north latitude. The tropic of Cancer, at 23.5° north latitude, divides the country in two. India therefore lies in the Tropics and subtropics. Most of the country is affected by the monsoon seasons, but there is also desert and tropical rain forest.

RAINFALL

In the far northwest, the low-lying Thar or Great Indian Desert lies in Rajasthan. The whole of Rajasthan has a dry climate, with an annual rainfall averaging about 250mm in the east but only 130mm in the desert. Summer temperatures reach 50°C, but they can fall below freezing on nights in winter.

Rainfall increases east of Rajasthan. Most of Uttar Pradesh and Madhya Pradesh receive moderate amounts of rain, although they are very hot and dry in early summer. Still farther to the east, Bihar, West Bengal, Chhattisgarh and Orissa have a warm, wet climate. Kolkata receives 1,600mm of rain a year, most of it falling during the summer monsoon months, from July to September. Assam, to the east of Bangladesh, is very wet, and with an average

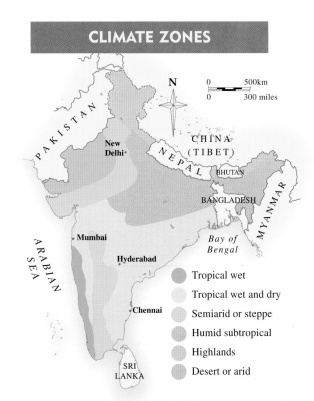

CLIMATE ZONES

N

0   500km
0   300 miles

PAKISTAN

New Delhi

CHINA (TIBET)

NEPAL

BHUTAN

BANGLADESH

Mumbai

ARABIAN SEA

Hyderabad

Bay of Bengal

MYANMAR

Chennai

SRI LANKA

- Tropical wet
- Tropical wet and dry
- Semiarid or steppe
- Humid subtropical
- Highlands
- Desert or arid

10,800mm of rain a year, the town of Cherrapunji is one of the wettest places on Earth. Dhubri, in lowland Assam, receives an average 2,525mm of rain a year – drier than Cherrapunji, but still with 4.5 times as much rain as falls on the famously rainy city of London.

The central part of the Deccan Plateau is fairly dry. Bangalore, the principal city of Karnataka, receives 900mm of rain a year. Surrounding the dry center, the main part of the Deccan has a moister but strongly seasonal climate.

MONSOON RAINS AND SEASONAL TEMPERATURES

The summer monsoon approaches India from the southwest. The western coastal plain of Maharashtra, Goa and Karnataka has a dry season lasting seven months but very heavy rainfall during the remainder of the year. Panaji in Goa receives 2,894mm of rain a year on average, but only 145mm falls between the beginning of November and the end of May. The coast of Kerala has a similar climate, but the dry season lasts for only three months. On the eastern coast, the wettest months are October, November and December.

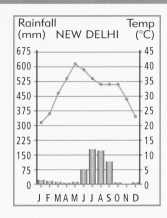

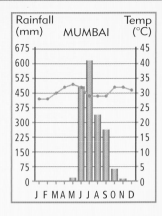

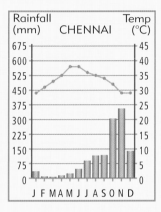

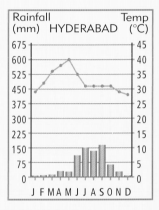

KEY:

Temperature

 Rainfall

Temperatures in Goa remain at about 26°C throughout the year. This is typical for places on the coast, where the proximity of the ocean moderates the temperature. Places inland experience a much wider range. Winter daytime temperatures in Delhi average 21°C, for example, but in early summer they exceed 40°C.

The landscape around Cherrapunji, Meghalaya, one of the rainiest places on Earth.

DISCARD

MONSOONS

The word *monsoon* comes from *mausim*, the Arabic word for "season." A monsoon climate is one with a very strong contrast between the seasons. That contrast is linked to a reversal in the direction of the prevailing winds. The change in wind direction that occurs over the Arabian Sea brings dry winters and wet summers to India and most of southern Asia.

In winter, central Asia becomes very cold. Cold, dense air sinks over the continent producing high surface air pressure. As the air sinks, however, it is compressed by the weight of air above it, and this makes its temperature rise. Air spills outward from the high-pressure region, sinks down the Himalayan ranges, and crosses India as a warm, dry wind from the northeast, bringing the dry winter monsoon season.

In summer, the land warms up much more quickly than the ocean and the pressure distribution reverses. Warm air rises over Central Asia, producing low pressure, while pressure remains relatively high over the cooler ocean. Air now flows across the ocean toward the land, gathering moisture as it does so.

This brings the wet summer monsoon, but the Asian monsoon is much stronger than monsoons elsewhere, because of the Himalayas. These form a barrier preventing the incoming air from moving farther north.

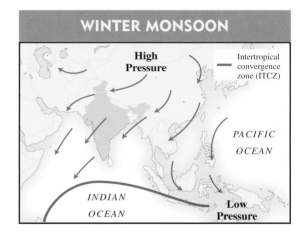

Connaught Place, New Delhi, at dusk, with dark clouds building overhead, promising monsoon rain.

Schoolboys share an umbrella as they walk home in the monsoon rain near Panvel, north of Mumbai.

It is April and in India the ground is parched and the air full of dust. Inland the temperature is rising, soon to pass 32°C during the day, with little relief at night. By May the nighttime temperature in Mumbai averages 27°C. This heat is bearable because the air is dry, but as May gives way to June, the humidity starts to rise. Clouds start to appear in the sky. They grow through the day, drifting from east to west, but dissipate by nightfall without bringing rain. Each day the clouds grow bigger and darker.

Then, in late June, the wind strengthens and starts to blow from the southwest. Suddenly the black skies open and rain falls in torrents. People laugh and enjoy their soaking as all the dust is washed from the air and the temperature drops. This is called the "burst of monsoon." It is a very abrupt start to the wet summer monsoon. The date on which it happens tells everyone whether the monsoon has arrived on time and the intensity of the storms give an indication of whether the rain will be sufficient to produce a good harvest – or so heavy that the land will be flooded.

At the same time, the Tibetan Plateau heats up and air rises over it, producing high pressure at high altitude, with air flowing outward from it, and the intertropical convergence zone (ITCZ) moves to its summer position over the mountains. These events combine to generate a high-level east-to-west wind – the easterly jet stream – that intensifies the movement of air across the Arabian Sea.

The summer monsoon reaches southern India in June, with winds out of the southwest blowing at about 45km/h and bringing dark clouds and violent rainstorms. It moves steadily northwestward, reaching Pakistan around the middle of July. The rains continue through the summer, but from the middle of September they become less intense. The ITCZ moves south for the winter, the easterly jet stream dies, and pressure begins to build over Central Asia as the temperature falls. By the end of December the dry winter monsoon is becoming established.

WHY THE TRADE WINDS ARE WET WINDS

Blowing on either side of the equator, the trade winds are the most reliable winds in the world. They blow from the northeast in the Northern Hemisphere and from the southeast in the Southern Hemisphere, gathering moisture as they cross the warm, tropical ocean.

The trade winds from both hemispheres meet at the intertropical convergence zone (ITCZ), where air rises, water vapor condenses to form clouds, and there are heavy and frequent rains. The ITCZ moves with the seasons. In the northern summer it lies at about 25° north latitude over Asia, crossing northern India and bringing heavy rain. Kolkata receives 950mm of rain between the beginning of June and the end of August. London receives less than 600mm in the entire year.

A fisherman and his daughters pray for rain standing on the dry bed of Lake Usmansagar in Hyderabad, Andhra Pradesh, emptied by severe drought.

EXTREMES OF WEATHER
MONSOON FAILURE

Indian farmers depend on the monsoon rains. If the rains arrive on time and in the usual amounts, the farmers can sow their crops knowing there will be enough water to enable the crops to ripen. If the rains arrive late the crops may have too little time to ripen and the harvest will be poor. If the monsoon fails altogether there will be no harvest at all and people will starve. For example, monsoon failures caused severe famine in 1877–78 and again in 1899–1900. An estimated 5 million people died during the 1877–78 famine. Chennai (formerly Madras) then had a population of 19.4 million, of whom 3.5 million died from hunger and disease. That famine followed an even worse famine in western India lasting from 1868 to 1870 when, in some areas, between one quarter and one third of the population perished. During the 1899–1900 famine, 1.25 million starved and 2 million died from disease.

Between 1965 and 1967, there was a severe drought in Bihar that caused a famine in which 1.5 million people died. However, that was the last occasion on which a failure of the monsoon resulted in tragedy on such a scale. In 1987, India suffered the most widespread drought to hit the country for a century, and in some parts of Gujarat and Rajasthan it was the third year in succession that the monsoon had failed. Relief supplies of food, water and livestock feed were distributed and there was no large-scale famine.

VIOLENT WEATHER

When the rains arrive they often arrive violently, with torrential storms that can wash away hillsides to cause landslides and mud slides. A short time later, as the deluge draining from the hills fills the tributaries, lowland rivers overflow their banks. That is when floods drive people from their homes and drown farm crops. Too much rain is just as bad as too little.

ABOVE: People traveling along a flooded road in Bihar after heavy monsoon rains caused the Bagmati River to overflow in September 2003.

BELOW: A man retrieves the roof of his home in Nadia village, Assam, after it was blown off during the April 2003 storm.

THE APRIL 2003 STORM

Even a single storm can cause appalling damage. On the night of 22 April 2003, a storm swept through the Dhubri district of Assam. By the morning at least 45 people had been killed and 4,000 injured, most of them when their thatched houses collapsed onto them or when they were struck by corrugated iron roofs torn from houses by the wind.

That storm gave warning of what lay ahead, as unusually heavy summer rains began to take their toll. In July, Rashid Ahmed, an Assamese farmer, told reporters: "I've lost my home and agricultural land. Not only mine, around 10 to 12 villages have already been submerged in the floods. . . . We have become beggars now." In fact, more than 3,000 villages in Assam were under water.

Assam was not the only state to suffer. Large areas of Himachal Pradesh, Bihar, West Bengal, Orissa and Arunachal Pradesh were also inundated, as well as parts of Pakistan and Bangladesh. Millions of people were made homeless and hundreds lost their lives.

Then, as the mud-laden rivers carried sewage through the streets and houses, waterborne diseases began to spread. Cholera, diarrhea, malaria and other diseases affected hundreds of thousands of people. It was October before the rains eased and the waters began to subside.

Rush hour on a street crowded with people in Chandni Chowk, New Delhi.

At midnight on 1 March 2001, the census recorded the population of India as 531,277,078 males and 495,738,169 females – a total of 1,027,015,247, making India the second most populous country in the world, after China.

DISTRIBUTION AND STRUCTURE

India's population is not distributed evenly. More people live on each square kilometer of land in the fertile Deccan than in the northern mountains, for example. On average, only 13.03 people live in every square kilometer of Arunachal Pradesh and 76.17 in Sikkim, but each square kilometer supports 835.47 people in Bihar and 819.25 in Kerala.

Between 1991 and 2001, the Indian population increased by 21.34 percent. Indians now make up one sixth of the world's population, and one third of them are less than 15 years old. India's population will continue to increase as the young reach their reproductive years.

TOTAL FERTILITY RATE

Women must each bear an average of 2.1 surviving children during the course of their lives if a population is to remain the same size.

The number of children that women produce is known as the total fertility rate (TFR). A TFR greater than 2.1 means the population will increase, and a TFR less than 2.1 means numbers will decrease.

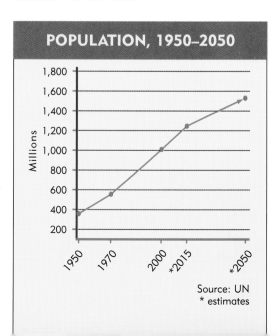

POPULATION, 1950–2050

Millions

1,800
1,600
1,400
1,200
1,000
800
600
400
200

1950 1970 2000 *2015 *2050

Source: UN
* estimates

POPULATION STRUCTURE, 2004

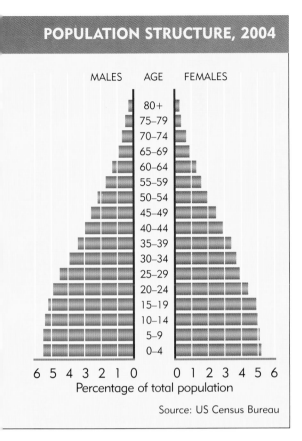

MALES   AGE   FEMALES

80+
75–79
70–74
65–69
60–64
55–59
50–54
45–49
40–44
35–39
30–34
25–29
20–24
15–19
10–14
5–9
0–4

6 5 4 3 2 1 0   0 1 2 3 4 5 6

Percentage of total population

Source: US Census Bureau

POPULATION DENSITY

Population per km²
- more than 1000
- 501–999
- 251–500
- 100–250
- less than 100

LIFE EXPECTANCY AT BIRTH

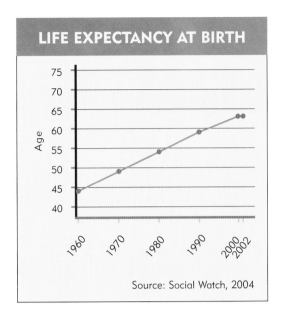

Source: Social Watch, 2004

UNDER-FIVE MORTALITY RATE

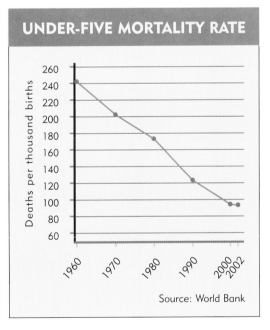

Source: World Bank

In India the TFR has been falling steadily for several years – from 3.11 in 2000 to 2.91 in 2003. If it continues to decrease at this rate it will reach 2.1 in about 2020. It is already at or below 2.1 in nine states and territories, and between 3.0 and 2.1 in a further 11. But the population will continue to increase for some time after 2020, because the number of women will increase as today's girls grow up.

ETHNIC GROUPS AND REGIONS

The Indian constitution recognizes 18 languages, but there are about 180 languages and probably hundreds of dialects. Each region has its own predominant language. The diversity of languages reflects the great variety of Indian peoples.

People in the north are generally tall, slim and light-skinned, while those in the south tend to be darker-skinned and of stockier build. There are people in Orissa who resemble Australian Aborigines, and people with East Asian features in the north and northeast.

Haryana and Punjab are the center of the Sikh religion, but they were also where the Mughal Empire began. The architecture and traditions show the mixture of Muslim and Hindu influences that merge in Sikhism.

Himachal Pradesh, in the hills to the north, is not far from Tibet. Dharamsala is the home of exiled Tibetans and the base of their

ABOVE: Women in Tamil Nadu. These are darker-skinned southerners who speak Tamil.

BELOW: A family traveling by rickshaw in New Delhi. These are lighter-skinned northerners who speak Hindi.

spiritual leader, the Dalai Lama. In the snow-covered hills, Buddhist prayer flags and monasteries are dotted among the Hindu temples and monuments. There are also Christian churches and many buildings that look European, because this is the region where Europeans used to retreat from the intense summertime heat of the plains.

Madhya Pradesh and Chhattisgarh are at the heart of Hindu India and have some of India's finest temples. The region was once Muslim, however, and a center for the Mughals, who ruled India from 1526 to 1707. Before that it was Buddhist. There are splendid Buddhist monuments not far from Bhopal in Madhya Pradesh. Chhattisgarh, in the southeast, is densely forested and very different in character. Its people are predominantly tribal.

For centuries, the states occupying the southern part of the Deccan had armies powerful enough to deter northern invaders.

CASE STUDY
THE ANDAMAN ISLANDERS

Far out in the Bay of Bengal, about 1,000km from the mainland, the 306 Andaman Islands are blanketed in tropical forest, with mangrove forest along the shores and coral reefs offshore. They are also the home of several tribes, including the Jarawas, Great Andamanese, Onges and Sentinelese. The Andaman Islanders are short and dark-skinned with tight, curly hair. They are related to African peoples.

On 26 December 2004, an undersea earthquake off northwestern Indonesia triggered tsunamis that swept across Sri Lanka, southeastern India and parts of Thailand and Indonesia. The waves swamped all of the Andaman and Nicobar Islands. When the waters subsided, nearly 2,000 Andamanese and Nicobarese were dead and a further 5,500 were missing, presumed dead.

This helped to isolate Tamil Nadu in the south. Southern Indians look different from northerners, speak what are known as Dravidian languages, and have developed their own Hindu culture. The finest, most ornate Hindu temples are in Tamil Nadu.

LANGUAGE FAMILIES
More than half the Indian population speak one of 11 Indo-European languages (a family of languages from Europe, India, and parts of Asia). The most important are Hindi, Urdu, Bengali and Marathi. Hindi and Urdu are written using different scripts, but they are very similar and share many words.

Hindi is spoken in and around Delhi. People in Kolkata speak Bengali. In Mumbai they speak Marathi. Tamil is spoken in Chennai. In Kerala people speak Malayalam.

TRIBES
Tribal people live mainly in the Himalayas, in the hills of the Deccan and in Bihar and West Bengal, but there are some tribes living in most states. Tribes vary in size from about 7.4 million Gonds, living in central India, to fewer than 20 Chaimals in the Andaman Islands. Members of recognized tribes receive special benefits and privileges from the central government.

A gypsy woman at a market in Margao, Goa, selling traditional jewelry she has made, similar to the jewelry she is wearing.

RELIGION

India is a land of temples and religious festivals. Religion plays a central role in Indian life. Although most people are Hindus, there are also Muslims, Christians, Sikhs and others. India was also the birthplace of Buddhism, although this is now a minority religion there.

HINDUISM

Hinduism is a religion of many deities and colorful rituals. It emerged about 2000 B.C., and today 74 percent of Indians are Hindu. There is no founder or single scriptural

A holy elephant blessing pilgrims inside the Minakshi Sundareshvara Temple, in Madurai, Tamil Nadu. The elephant's markings symbolize the Hindu god Vishnu.

authority for Hindu beliefs, but the main tenets of the religion are set out in seven texts called the Vedas. Two key aspects are adherence to dharma (divine law) and belief in reincarnation. The later Vedas describe a social category of people, called Brahmans, who specialize in interpreting and teaching the texts and conducting rituals.

THE CASTE SYSTEM

In India, social status was traditionally inherited and every individual belonged to one of the thousands of occupational groups, or castes. The castes were grouped into four ranks called *varnas*. Brahmans, most of them priests or scholars, held the highest rank. Kshatriyas, rulers and soldiers, came next, followed by Sudras, who were laborers, peasants, craftspeople and domestic servants. Finally the "untouchables," now called Dalits, performed the most menial and degrading tasks. The social hierarchy based on the caste system was developed by the northerners. Indians are now trying hard to break down the barriers it imposes.

In modern India it is illegal to discriminate against someone on the basis of that person's caste, and affirmative action is practiced to help members of the lower castes enter higher education and government employment. Despite this, remnants of the caste system still survive.

RELIGIONS

Traditional religions 3.4%
Sikh 2.0%
Buddhist 0.7%
Jain 0.4%
Other 1.5%
Christian 6.0%
Muslim 12.0%
Hindu 74.0%

Source: Census of India, 2001

Pilgrims crossing the courtyard of the Sikh Golden Temple at Amritsar, Punjab, seen from a colonnaded passage.

Slightly more than 6 percent of the population are Christian. St Thomas the Apostle may have brought Christianity to India in the first century A.D., but it spread following the arrival of Vasco da Gama in 1498 and St Francis Xavier in 1542. Many of the Dalits (who are sometimes called "untouchables") and tribal people are Christians.

ISLAM AND CHRISTIANITY

Islam, which entered India in the seventh and eighth centuries with Arab, Persian and Turkish invaders, recognizes only one god and opposes the worship of idols. Its central teachings are set forth in the Qur'an (or Koran) and the Sunnah. Today about 12 percent of Indians are Muslim.

A large crowd of Muslims gathered outside a mosque.

JAINISM, BUDDHISM AND SIKHISM

Jainism was founded in around 599 B.C. Jains aim to lead a simple, pure life, avoiding violence to any person and, so far as possible, to any living being. In this way they hope to escape the cycle of birth, death and rebirth.

Founded by Siddartha Gautama, who was born in 566 B.C. in what is now Nepal, Buddhism regards all people as equals. It spread widely in northern and central India, and Buddhist monasteries became seats of learning and centers of education. By the eighth century A.D., however, Buddhist influence was waning in India. At the same time it was spreading throughout other parts of Asia.

During the fifteenth century, when India was under Muslim rule, the Sikh religion emerged as a reaction against both Islam and Brahmanism. Sikhs believe in one god and reject the caste system and the worship of idols, but they believe in karma and the cycle of birth and rebirth, which are derived from Hinduism. Sikh men are recognizable by their beards and the turbans they wear to cover their hair, which they must never cut.

EDUCATION

Before British rule in India, which began early in the nineteenth century, only the sons of high-status families received a formal education. Others were trained for the jobs appropriate to their social position (see caste system box on page 28). The British needed civil servants to help run the country, so they introduced the British educational system, setting up schools modeled on those in England and extending education to the daughters of high-status families.

LITERACY

Most people remained illiterate, however. The 1951 census, taken several years after British rule ended in 1947, found that only 27 percent of males and 9 percent of females were able to read and write, giving an overall literacy rate of 18.3 percent.

Girls in a class studying outdoors at a rural school in Bodh Gaya, Bihar.

CASE STUDY
RURAL SCHOOLS

The Rural Development Foundation (RDF) is one of many nongovernmental organizations that run free schools throughout rural India.

One such school is in Kalleda village in Andhra Pradesh. The RDF and a village committee manage the school for 200 children from kindergarten to age 11. Meals are provided free and the school also supplies uniforms to eliminate caste and class distinctions. Students are selected by a lottery to ensure fairness.

Matendla, also in Andhra Pradesh, is considered an undeveloped area. With financial support from the India Literacy Project and the American Telugu Association, the RDF runs Matendla Rural School, which will eventually have 350 students up to age 12.

Young men learning to use computers at the Raghabir Nagar community center, New Delhi.

Although India has made great strides since that time, the government's goal of compulsory free education for everyone has not yet been attained. Many government schools are very short of basic equipment such as chalkboards, books and furniture. Today approximately 75 percent of males and 55 percent of females are literate – 65.2 percent of the total population – although literacy is much higher in urban than in rural areas. There are also geographic differences. In Kerala, almost 90 percent of people are literate, but less than than 50 percent are literate in Bihar.

The Indian government attaches great importance to the improvement of the education system, and for very practical reasons. Studies have shown that if farmers receive four years of elementary schooling their productivity increases by an average 8.5 percent, and the introduction in the 1960s of high-yield "green revolution" crops and

technologies is known to have proceeded faster among educated farmers. Education is a crucial component in the struggle to eliminate hunger. Education also reduces inequalities and increases the share of national income earned by the poorest people. Obviously, as high-technology industries expand, the need for a skilled, educated workforce will continue to grow.

PRIMARY, MIDDLE AND SECONDARY SCHOOLING

Indian schools are run by the states but financed by central government. Children attend primary school from age 6 to 14. This is free and officially compulsory, with about 90 percent of all children enrolling at primary school. But many do not attend regularly. Only about half of all children age 11 to 14 enroll at middle school. Parents must pay for their children's secondary education up to the age of 18, and only about 20 percent of young people enroll.

HIGHER EDUCATION

For the few who go on to higher education, India now has nearly 230 universities and many more agricultural, technical and other colleges. Indian scientists are engaged in world-class research across a wide range of disciplines. For example, India has a space program and maintains several communications and meteorological satellites.

University students in Chennai.

URBAN INDIA

India possesses some of the world's greatest, most beautiful and, in places, most crowded cities. Despite the size of its major cities, India is not heavily urbanized, and about 70 percent of the population live in villages of fewer than 5,000 inhabitants.

The pattern is changing, however. As the economy develops, manufacturing industries and commerce expand. This generates urban jobs that pay wages higher than those people can earn working on farms. At the same time, the modernization of agriculture eliminates some farmworkers' jobs. Displaced or attracted by hopes of a better life, more and more people move into the cities. This happens everywhere and India is no exception, but in India the pace of urbanization is slow. In 1981, 23.7 percent of Indians lived in urban areas. This figure increased to 25.7 percent in 1991 and by 2001 it had reached 27.8 percent – little more than one quarter of the population.

CASE STUDY
SLUMS IN KOLKATA

About 1.5 million people in Kolkata live in slums, like this one beside a canal.

Between 1981 and 2001, the population of the Kolkata metropolitan area grew more than 40 percent from 9.1 million to 13.2 million, and the city has been unable to cope. Of the 4.6 million inhabitants of the city itself, about 1.5 million live in slums. A slum is defined as an area with more than 25 temporary homes, called *katcha* buildings.

In registered slums, called *bustees*, residents own or rent the ground on which they erect their homes. There may be as many as 500 *katchas* in a bustee. Unregistered slums, which have sprung up along roadsides, beside canals, and on vacant ground, offer no such security. Kolkata has 2,011 *bustees* and 3,500 unregistered slums.

Three quarters of the slum population live below the poverty line. Many are unemployed. Others work as ragpickers, rickshaw-pullers, and casual laborers. Kolkata Municipal Corporation is striving to provide these areas with a clean water supply, sanitation, waste disposal facilities, street lighting, schools and better employment prospects.

URBAN POPULATION

% of total population

36	
34	
32	
30	
28	
26	
24	
22	
20	
18	
16	
14	

1950 1970 2000 *2015

Source: UN
* estimate

Indian cities are overwhelmed by the growth in traffic and population. Traffic on this street in Old Delhi is gridlocked.

LIFE IN THE CITY

The new city dwellers maintain close links with their home villages. It is usually a man who moves to the city, often alone but sometimes accompanied by his wife and children. He keeps in touch with his parents, brothers, sisters, uncles, aunts, cousins, nieces and nephews back in the village, visiting when he can and sending them money. If he succeeds in his new life, other family members may follow his lead.

Many of those moving into the cities set up their own businesses making and selling craft goods, running shops, driving taxis, or providing some other service. Not everyone succeeds, however, and many people are in poorly paid jobs, work only intermittently or can find no work at all. The poor live in squalid, overcrowded slums that contrast starkly with the modern apartment buildings and spacious houses of the rich.

Although the rate of urbanization is slow, the Indian population is so large that this migration has greatly increased the size of the urban population. India's largest city, including the surrounding urban area, is Mumbai (Bombay). The population of the

Mumbai metropolitan area, has doubled in 20 years, from 8.2 million in 1981 to 16.4 million in 2001. Other Indian cities have expanded at similar rates.

Rapid urban expansion has severely strained city services. Public transport is crowded and traffic jams are common. Cities are struggling to provide adequate sewers, storm drains to carry away rainwater, and a reliable supply of clean water. Education and health services have difficulty coping with the demands made on them.

Brigade Road in the "electronic city" of Bangalore, Karnataka, where neon signs and bright shop fronts attract passersby.

Two women carrying loads on their heads walk past the parliament building in New Delhi.

In 1858 Indian territories formerly controlled by the British East India Company were made part of the British Empire. Most of India was then ruled by the British and Queen Victoria became Empress of India. After a long struggle, India won back its independence in 1947.

India is sometimes described as the world's largest democracy, and in April and May 2004 it held the world's largest election. Nearly 380 million people voted (out of an electorate of 675 million) and polling took place on four separate days as officials moved 1 million voting machines to locations in different states.

THE PRESIDENT AND THE PRIME MINISTER

India's president is the head of state. He or she has certain powers, such as declaring states of emergency and calling on the leader of the political party with the greatest parliamentary support to form a government. In practice, the president is rarely able to act except on the advice of the government.

A mother feeds her child in front of an election poster for Sonia Gandhi, leader of the Congress Party, on a street in Lucknow, Uttar Pradesh.

The prime minister heads the government, choosing the members of his or her cabinet from among elected members of parliament. The prime minister, cabinet and junior ministers oversee the running of the country. The judges and courts of law are independent of the government.

THE HOUSES OF PARLIAMENT

India's legislature consists of two houses of parliament. The lower house, called the Lok Sabha or People's Assembly, has 545 members. Citizens age 18 and older elect 543 for five-year terms, and the president appoints two. The upper house, called the Rajya Sabha or Council of States, has 250 members. The president appoints 12 individuals who have made distinguished contributions to national life, and the state assemblies elect 238.

On the recommendation of the prime minister, the president appoints the governors of each of the 28 states. The governor is the state equivalent of the national president. Local governments exist at the city, town, district and village level.

REDRAWING STATE BOUNDARIES

At the time of independence in 1947, India's state boundaries took little account of local cultures and languages. During the 1950s, demands grew for the boundaries to be redrawn on a linguistic basis, so that a single language would predominate in each state. In 1952 Andhra Pradesh, where Telugu is the most widely spoken language, became the first linguistically defined state. In the 1950s and 1960s, several other such states were created, including Tamil Nadu, Kerala and Gujarat, for Tamil, Malayalam and Gujarati speakers respectively.

CASE STUDY
THE DIVISION OF PUNJAB

Sikh men, easily recognizable by their turbans and beards, on a street in Punjab.

Punjab to create what were known as the Himalayan Provinces. These are now called Himachal Pradesh, which became a state in 1966 with its capital at Shimla.

Indian Punjab was further divided in 1966 to separate the region where most people follow the Sikh religion from the predominantly Hindu region. The Sikh region is the modern state of Punjab and the Hindu region is the state of Haryana. Punjabi is the predominant language in Punjab and Hindi in Haryana.

The Indian states of Punjab and Haryana were once part of a much larger territory called Punjab. At independence, Punjab was divided into two approximately equal parts, one lying inside India and the other in Pakistan. Territories were then removed from Indian

Punjab and Haryana share the same capital, Chandigarh, which was specially built in the 1950s to a design by the Swiss architect Le Corbusier. Since the city is the capital of two states and belongs exclusively to neither of them, it is classed as a union territory, governed directly by the central government.

KASHMIR

Kashmir, in the far north of India, was once one of the princely states, consisting of Kashmir itself with its summer capital at Srinagar, Ladakh in the east bordering Tibet, and the district around the winter capital of Jammu in the southwest. The great majority of the people were Muslim, but Hindus and Sikhs formed a majority around Jammu, and Ladakh was predominantly Buddhist.

At independence in 1947, the rulers of all the princely states were allowed to choose whether their territories should become part of India or of Pakistan. Hari Singh, the Hindu maharajah of Kashmir, hesitated and in October 1947 tribesmen crossed the border from Muslim Pakistan, headed for Srinagar, and occupied about 40 percent of the territory. Faced with the prospect of losing his kingdom, Hari Singh decided that Kashmir should become part of India and he appealed to New Delhi for help. Indian troops were flown to Srinagar and after fierce fighting the tribesmen were forced to retreat.

The UN intervened in the dispute. It negotiated a cease-fire and called for a plebiscite – a vote of the entire population – to decide Kashmir's future.

Srinagar, the summer capital of Jammu and Kashmir, is a city of lakes, gardens, and beautiful wooden buildings.

In 1949 a cease-fire line was drawn, placing 38 percent of Kashmir on the Pakistani side and 62 percent on the Indian side. The plebiscite has still not been held and both India and Pakistan continue to lay claim to the entire region.

SPECIAL STATUS FOR KASHMIR

In order to persuade the people of both parts of Kashmir to join India, Article 370 of the Indian constitution gives Kashmir special status, allowing it to make its own laws and run its own affairs in all matters except for defense, foreign affairs and communications.

The status of Kashmir remains undecided. Some people accuse India of persistently interfering in Kashmiri politics, thus undermining the state's autonomy, and of promoting the interests of the Hindu minority at the expense of the Muslim majority. Certain Kashmiri groups want union with Pakistan while others would like Kashmir to become an independent country. Within India there are Hindu groups, including the Bharitaya Janata Party, which maintain that Kashmir is an

Wagah, on the border between Indian and Pakistani Kashmir. Every day Pakistani rangers (right) try to beat the Indian border police in a race to lower their flags and close the border.

integral part of India and is not entitled to special status. The organizations calling for Kashmiri independence boycotted the elections that were held in 1996.

Pakistan continues to assert its claim on Kashmir and supports militant groups fighting inside Kashmir. India is thus compelled to maintain large military and paramilitary forces in the area. Kashmir is the scene of a low-level war that, from time to time, escalates into a direct confrontation between India and Pakistan. Thousands of lives have been lost and most Hindus have left the worst-affected areas.

CASE STUDY
WAR AND NUCLEAR CONFRONTATION

Congress Party supporters marching through Kolkata to urge the government to take action against Pakistan over Kashmir.

Fighting over Kashmir has broken out between India and Pakistan in 1947, 1965 and 1999. The 1947 war began when tribal fighters crossed into Kashmir from Pakistan. In 1965 Pakistan-backed guerrillas infiltrated Kashmir, leading to skirmishes with Indian troops and retaliation from Pakistan that escalated into war. In 1999 conflict began when Pakistani troops in civilian dress infiltrated north of the city of Kargil, establishing positions from which they could shell various targets and from which they were driven mainly by air attacks.

Since 1998 there have been fears that nuclear weapons might be used in future wars. India conducted an underground nuclear test in 1974 and on 11 May 1998 tested three nuclear devices in Rajasthan. The newly elected Bharatiya Janata Party government then declared India to be a nuclear-weapon power. Between 28 and 30 May, Pakistan responded by carrying out six nuclear weapon tests.

FOREIGN RELATIONS

India became independent of British rule and established good relations with the United Kingdom. France also held territories in India, and control of these was also handed over peacefully. Portugal, however, refused to relinquish its territories of Goa, now a state, and the towns of Damão (now Daman) and Diu, which are now union territories. In December 1961 India took these territories by force.

India is a republic but remains a member of the Commonwealth, an international organization headed by the British monarch.

NONALIGNED MOVEMENT

Jawaharlal Nehru, India's first prime minister, was determined that India should play an active international role. He wanted India to be able to mediate between the Western and Communist blocs by pursuing a policy of "nonalignment." India encouraged other Asian nations to unite around their common interests and, in 1955, took part in a conference of 29 Asian and African nations held in Bandung, Indonesia. The Bandung Conference established the nonaligned group of nations, of which India is still a prominent member.

India, then a British territory, was a founding member of the United Nations in 1945 and actively supports it today. India has contributed more than 55,000 military and civilian police to 35 UN peacekeeping operations, as well as troops, paramedics and observers to UN forces. It has also chaired several UN commissions set up to implement cease-fire agreements. The Indian Army has helped to clear mines in Rwanda, Mozambique, Somalia, Angola and Cambodia.

CHINA, THE SOVIET UNION AND THE UNITED STATES

Nehru tried but failed to establish warm relations with China, and in 1962 the two countries fought a war that India lost. This led India to seek stronger ties with the Soviet Union, largely to counterbalance the ties Pakistan was developing with China and the United States. Later, as the Cold War continued, US relations with China improved and the United States became the major provider of aid and arms to Pakistan, driving India even closer to the Soviet Union. When Soviet forces occupied Afghanistan in the 1980s, the United States supported the Afghan resistance, based in Pakistan.

Today the United States is India's biggest trading partner, and US support for Pakistan has weakened following the end of the Cold War. But US relations with India remain strained due to India's possession of nuclear weapons and its refusal to sign the Nuclear Non-Proliferation Treaty (because of the failure of the five original signatories to destroy their own nuclear stockpiles).

An Indian UN patrol near Ghajar village on the border between Israel and South Lebanon.

Tibetan Buddhist monks, refugees at Dharamsala, Himachal Pradesh.

India recognized the Communist government in China in 1949 and sought friendly relations. But it condemned the Chinese invasion of Tibet in 1950 and said it would defend the border states of Nepal, Bhutan and Sikkim.

In March 1959 the Chinese suppressed a Tibetan uprising. India did not condemn the suppression but gave shelter to the Dalai Lama and large numbers of Tibetan refugees. Then in August 1959 Chinese troops occupied northeastern India and China asserted territorial claims in the region.

Consultations failed to resolve the issue. In 1962 China invaded and Chinese forces advanced quickly, overrunning Indian positions, but then withdrew. There were further clashes in 1967, but China did not intervene in the 1971 Indo-Pakistani War.

Former prime ministers Atal Behari Vajpayee of India and Zhu Rongji of China in New Delhi.

Farmworkers winnowing rice – sorting the grain from the chaff – in Tamil Nadu.

India is modernizing its economy. Manufacturing and service industries provide an increasing proportion of the total number of jobs. Nevertheless, most Indians continue to live in villages and rural areas, and agriculture remains by far the most important national industry. Two thirds of all Indians work on the land, either on farms or in forests.

Between them, agriculture and forestry generate approximately 25 percent of India's gross domestic product (GDP), yet they account for 65 percent of the workforce. Almost every part of India is farmed, and land under permanent crop cultivation accounts for more than 57 percent of the country's total land area. Areas set aside as wildlife refuges, the Thar Desert, beaches and steep, rocky mountain slopes together occupy about 16 percent of the land area; forests 23 percent; pasture and meadows almost 4 percent; and urban and built-up areas, such as roads, 0.2 percent.

CROPS

Wheat and rice are the most important staple foods – those that provide the bulk of what people eat. Wheat is grown on the western

AGRICULTURE

N

0   500km
0   300 miles

PAKISTAN

CHINA
(TIBET)

NEPAL   BHUTAN

BANGLADESH

MYANMAR

Bay of
Bengal

ARABIAN
SEA

Millets

Wheat

Rice

SRI
LANKA

DIET (% OF CALORIES DERIVED FROM VARIOUS FOODS)

Fruit and vegetables 3.2%

Other 18.2%

Fats and oils 8.5%

Cereals 62.7%

Eggs and milk 4.5%

Fish 0.4%

Meat and poultry 0.9%

Potatoes 1.6%

Source: Government of India Central Statistical Organisation

THE GREEN REVOLUTION AND RISING YIELDS

India benefited greatly from the introduction of new varieties of wheat and rice, along with increased use of fertilizer and better irrigation, during the so-called green revolution of the 1960s, and yields continue to rise. Average wheat yields between 1995 and 2000 were 40 percent higher than between 1971 and 1980. Rice yields rose by 65 percent during the same period.

The increase in output means that India now produces enough food for its population. According to the Food and Agriculture Organization (FAO) of the United Nations, Indians now receive 112 percent of the recommended minimum number of calories per day. This is an average figure, however, and conceals the fact that while some sections of society eat very well there are others who often go hungry.

In all countries where agriculture is the most important industry, wages are low and people are poor. India is no exception. More than 50 percent of the average household income is spent on food. In the United States, this figure is 10 percent.

side of the Deccan Plateau and across northern India, extending well into the Himalayan foothills. Rice is grown throughout the country.

Sorghum and millet are also grown widely. These produce seeds that are ground into flour that can be cooked to make a kind of porridge or baked as unleavened bread. Some varieties of sorghum have a sweet-tasting stem, rather like sugarcane.

In addition to cereal crops, Indian farmers grow sugarcane, tea and coffee. Sugarcane grows on lower ground over much of the country. Tea grows best in the hills of northeastern India, especially in Assam, which produces more than half of all Indian tea, and the hills around Darjiling, West Bengal. Tea is also grown in southwestern India, in Karnataka and Kerala. Coffee is grown mainly in Karnataka.

Picking tea on a plantation in the hills near Darjiling, West Bengal.

HOUSEHOLD EXPENDITURE (% OF TOTAL INCOME)

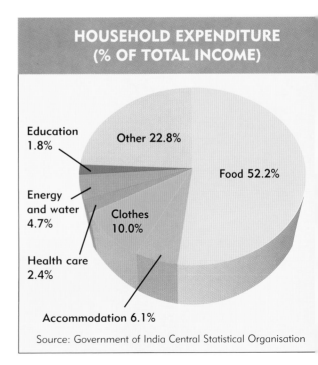

Education 1.8%

Other 22.8%

Food 52.2%

Energy and water 4.7%

Clothes 10.0%

Health care 2.4%

Accommodation 6.1%

Source: Government of India Central Statistical Organisation

IRRIGATION

Indian farmers rely on the monsoon rains that supply approximately three quarters of the country's annual rainfall. The monsoon is unreliable, however, and the water it delivers falls so rapidly that a great deal runs off and is lost before plant roots can absorb it. Irrigation provides water when it is needed, rather than when the climate delivers it, and making water available at the right time can dramatically increase yields.

Two thirds of Indian farmland is watered only by the rain, and one third is irrigated. Artificial reservoirs held behind dams provide water for all uses, and more dams are being planned and built. About five sixths of the water held in these reservoirs is used for crop irrigation. Despite the gains achieved in recent decades, the average yield of Indian cereal crops is still less than half that in China and the United States. Expanding the area of irrigated land and improving farming techniques could raise Indian yields to these levels.

TRADITIONAL IRRIGATION

Traditionally, irrigation water is lifted from a well or river by means of either a bucket-and-pole device or a wheel. The bucket-and-pole, known in India as a *denkli* or *paecottah*, consists of a long, tapering pole mounted on a crossbeam. A bucket hangs from one end and the other end is counterweighted. A worker pulls on a rope to lower the bucket into the well. When the bucket is full, releasing the rope allows it to rise.

The wheel, called a *harat*, is mounted on a horizontal axis. It carries buckets that fill at the bottom and empty their contents into irrigation channels at the top. Mechanical pumps are tending to replace these ancient devices.

Surplus irrigation water must be allowed to drain away. If it accumulates the land may

Irrigation on farmland in Punjab. Water pumped from the ground flows through a system of channels that take it to the fields.

Hindus drink milk and eat butter and other dairy products, but they will not permit cattle to be killed for food and they will not eat beef. Cows are allowed to walk through the streets. When a family buys a new cow, its legs are ritually washed and it is welcomed into the home with a religious ceremony.

Cows are sacred because they are so useful. They provide milk, so they resemble human mothers. Oxen, the males, pull the plough and other farm implements, helping the farmer to produce food for his family. Cow dung fertilizes the soil.

The religious significance is deeper, however. Krishna, an incarnation of the god Vishnu, was a cowherd and played his flute to

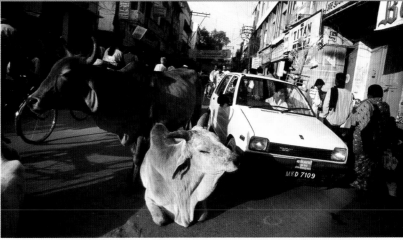

Cows holding up the rush-hour traffic on a main road in Varanasi, Uttar Pradesh.

the cows in his charge. In one story, a cow called Kamadhenu gave milk to Vishnu. Every Hindu god has an animal companion and Shiva, the destroyer of evil, rides on a bull called Nandhi.

become waterlogged and the evaporation of surface water will leave behind dissolved salts that slowly poison the land – a process called salinization. Large areas of Indian cropland have suffered from waterlogging and salinization.

LIVESTOCK

Besides plant crops, Indian farmers also raise livestock. Each year, India produces about 400 million chickens, 94 million water buffalo, more than 1 million camels, 123 million goats, 58 million sheep, 16 million pigs and a staggering 219 million cattle. Water buffalo, oxen and camels are working animals. The other species are raised for food, wool and skins. The chickens lay approximately 1.8 million tonnes of eggs each year and the cattle yield 22 million tonnes of milk.

Goatherds driving their animals along a road in Rajasthan. The animals are unperturbed by the passing trucks.

FORESTS

About 2,000 years ago, forests covered 85 percent of India. Many human communities lived in the forests and found all of their food and materials there. People managed the forests even then, by planting trees they found useful and clearing land to grow crops.

The situation changed during the nineteenth and twentieth centuries, when forests were cleared to provide farmland for more profitable crops. The rapid expansion of the railroads in the late nineteenth century consumed huge amounts of wood to make ties and to build stations. Satellite images show that today only 23 percent of India is forested. Large areas of forest are still being lost, mainly because of illegal cutting by local communities to provide land for raising livestock. At present, Indian forests produce approximately 303 million m^3 of wood a year, of which 279 million m^3 is fuelwood.

SOCIAL FORESTRY

Approximately one third of the Indian population – some 360 million people – live in or close to the forests. Nearly one fifth of those – 68 million people – are classed as tribal or indigenous peoples. These are among the poorest members of Indian society. Consequently, the forested areas have the highest density of tribal areas, and more than 60 per cent of the people living in the forests of Jharkhand,

The forests of Madhya Pradesh, seen from the highest point in the Satpura Range of hills.

West Bengal, Madhya Pradesh, Chhattisgarh and Orissa are below the poverty line. These are the people whose way of life depends on the forests.

Beginning with the Indian Forest Act of 1878, forests have been brought under the control of the central government. The rights

The home of a tribal family living in the forested hills of Meghalaya, in northeastern India.

of local communities to the produce of the forests, which they had enjoyed throughout their history, were redefined as privileges and then taken away altogether.

In recent years, the Indian government has recognized this problem. In 1976 it launched the Social Forestry Program (SFP) with the aim of satisfying the needs of local communities without compromising the supply of industrial timber. Most SFP projects were successful. Between 1950 and 1979, forests were being planted at an average rate of 0.11 million hectares a year. The rate rose to 1.3 million hectares a year between 1980 and 1989.

There were problems, however. In particular, the SFP suffered from an industrial bias. Villagers needed trees to supply fruit, fuel and fodder for their livestock. However, most plantations grew eucalyptus, which grows fast and produces high-quality timber for the construction industry, but no edible leaves or fruit.

FORESTS

Forest area

Students watering seedlings in a tree nursery in the Rishi Valley of Andhra Pradesh.

JOINT FOREST MANAGEMENT

Social forestry is now being replaced by Joint Forest Management (JFM). Its aim is to restore and regenerate up to 50 million hectares of degraded land. Forest projects are organized by local groups of 10 to 100 households, with the support of the state forest department. JFM does not transfer the ownership of the forests, most of which belong to the state, but it allows local communities to control access to the forests and to decide how they should be managed. The forests supply the needs of the villagers without harming the wild plants and animals.

The nuclear power station at Elephanta Island in Mumbai Harbor. India has six nuclear power stations and is increasing its use of nuclear power.

Although agriculture is the biggest industry in India, its importance is decreasing as the economy modernizes. The founders of independent India determined that the country would develop an advanced industrial economy. They planned the energy, transport, communications and financial structures that would support rapid industrialization. Industrialization would provide jobs and reduce poverty.

In 1950 agriculture, forestry and fisheries generated 59 percent of GDP, and manufacturing – mainly jute and cotton textiles – produced 10 percent. Today agriculture generates only 25 percent of GDP, while industry accounts for 25 percent and the service sector 50 percent.

This change has raised the standard of living, but it will be some time before Indian living standards match those in the West. Although more than 75 percent of urban homes have electric light and almost 64 percent have an indoor toilet, access to these facilities is much lower in rural areas where the majority of Indians live. Nationally, just over 40 percent of homes have electric light and less than 24 percent have an indoor toilet.

RESOURCES

India possesses the natural resources needed for industrialization. It has reserves of iron ore, chromite, lead, zinc, copper, bauxite (aluminum ore) and chromite (the principal chromium ore; chromium is used to make high-quality steel). To power its smelters, foundries and factories, India has reserves comprising more than 84 billion tonnes of coal, nearly 440 billion m^3 of natural gas, and 4.8 billion barrels of oil.

Fossil fuels generate 80 percent of the country's electricity, with hydroelectric plants

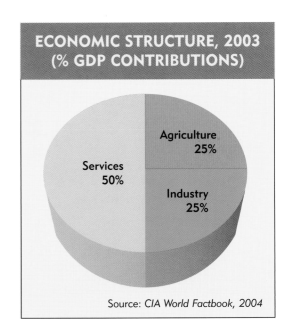

ECONOMIC STRUCTURE, 2003
(% GDP CONTRIBUTIONS)

Agriculture 25%

Services 50%

Industry 25%

Source: *CIA World Factbook, 2004*

providing about 16 percent. There is also a small contribution from nuclear power. In 2004 India had six nuclear power stations, with a total of 10 working reactors, and six more reactors were under construction.

NEW INDUSTRIES

Although traditional industries, such as textile manufacture, continue to provide a large amount of employment, they are no longer the most valuable industries. Whereas textiles contribute about Rs 100 billion to the economy each year, the manufacture of motor vehicles contributes Rs 120 billion and the chemical industry – making synthetic fibers, agrochemicals, drugs and medicines, paints, cosmetics and soaps – contributes Rs 237 billion.

These industries pay higher wages than the older industries. Workers in the agrochemical industry earn more than double the national average wage, and those working in oil refineries earn 3.5 times the average. Even so, wages are still low enough to attract foreign companies, and many Western organizations have relocated their call centers to India (see page 51). Rising prosperity, at least among high-paid workers, is stimulating the demand for leisure services, so this sector is also expanding.

Workers packing medicines at a pharmaceuticals factory in Mumbai.

THE BALANCE OF TRADE

Despite the economic progress India is making, the value of the country's imports continues to exceed that of its exports – by Rs 359 billion (about US $8 billion) in 2001–02. At present, jewelry and cut and polished diamonds provide 20 percent of India's export earnings, ready-made cotton garments 9 percent, and leather goods 4 percent. Oil is the biggest import.

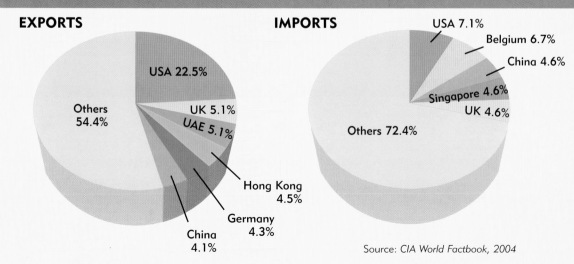

MAJOR TRADING PARTNERS (% OF VALUE), 2003

EXPORTS

USA 22.5%
Others 54.4%
UK 5.1%
UAE 5.1%
Hong Kong 4.5%
Germany 4.3%
China 4.1%

IMPORTS

USA 7.1%
Belgium 6.7%
China 4.6%
Singapore 4.6%
UK 4.6%
Others 72.4%

Source: *CIA World Factbook, 2004*

TRADITIONAL INDUSTRIES

Modern industries pay high wages, but some traditional industries employ far more workers, many of them highly skilled, producing goods that are exported all over the world. For example, approximately 20 million people work in the textile industry.

LUXURY FABRICS

Varanasi, on the banks of the Ganges in Uttar Pradesh, is one of the world's oldest cities and is sacred to both Hindus and Buddhists. It is also a center of textile production. For more than 2,000 years, weavers at Varanasi have been producing the finest cotton cloth, and since the sixteenth century they have been incorporating gold and silver threads to make luxurious brocades. Their richest cloths were traditionally made for royalty and exported to Tibetan monasteries, but the weavers also produce fine silk saris and scarves. Craft workers at Agra, also in Uttar Pradesh, use gold thread and beads to make *zardosi* – fabrics embroidered with elaborate designs.

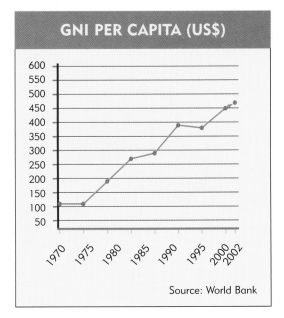

GNI PER CAPITA (US$)

Source: World Bank

TRIBAL CRAFTS

Craft products provide a useful income for many tribal people. The techniques and designs are part of tribal culture, but the beauty and vivid colors of the products ensure a ready demand for them.

Metal ornaments, especially those made from brass, are exported, as are items made from cane and carved wood. Craft workers also produce hand-knotted carpets.

Weaving silk to make saris on a hand loom in the old city of Varanasi, Uttar Pradesh.

This tribal woman in Sikkim is weaving a carpet with a traditional design.

Loading coal onto a truck at a strip mine in Bihar.

Reform of the Indian economy, which began in the late 1970s, is based on reducing state control. As part of this process, Indian coal mines are to be privatized. Labor unions fear that privatization will lead to lower wages and a return to poorer conditions.

India is also the world's largest producer of mica, used mainly for electrical insulation and to make windows for industrial furnaces, and a major producer of a range of other minerals. These resources are distributed throughout India and employ about 700,000 workers. The minerals industry contributes only about 2.5 percent of GDP, although it accounts for 10 to 11 percent of industrial GDP. When cut diamonds are excluded, mineral exports amount to only 3.1 percent of total exports.

COAL AND MINERALS – THE EXTRACTIVE INDUSTRIES

Not all of the traditional industries are so colorful. India has more than 500 coal mines, located in Assam, Bihar, West Bengal, Madhya Pradesh, Uttar Pradesh, Maharashtra, Orissa and Andhra Pradesh. India is the world's third-largest producer of hard coal (as opposed to brown coal or lignite), after the United States and China. Power stations are the biggest customers for Indian coal.

The coal industry has been state owned since the early 1970s, when it was nationalized. More than 90 percent of all coal production is controlled by Coal India Ltd (CIL), the state operating company.

Since nationalization, investment has increased and working conditions, which were once dangerous, have improved. CIL employs about 643,000 workers and since 1974–75 annual expenditure on welfare services and housing for miners has increased from Rs 200 million to Rs 11 billion.

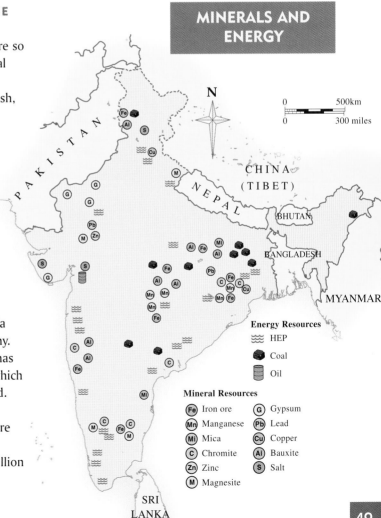

MINERALS AND ENERGY

Energy Resources
≋ HEP
◆ Coal
▮ Oil

Mineral Resources
Fe Iron ore
Mn Manganese
MI Mica
C Chromite
Zn Zinc
M Magnesite
G Gypsum
Pb Lead
Cu Copper
Al Bauxite
S Salt

MODERN INDUSTRIES

IRON AND STEEL

The iron and steel industry is important: As well as supplying the domestic market, it earns valuable foreign exchange through exports. Domestically, iron and steel are made into a wide range of machines and machine tools that are used in many industries. India also exports machinery.

THE MOTOR INDUSTRY

Indian factories have been making cars, motorcycles and commercial vehicles since the 1940s, and the motor industry is now very large. There are nearly 3,800 factories employing almost 400,000 people. In 2001–02 the industry produced more than 163,500 cars and sport-utility vehicles (SUVs), nearly 29,000 commercial vehicles and more than 1 million motorcycles and all-terrain vehicles (ATVs). Many of these were exported, mainly to Latin America and Eastern Europe.

Foreign manufacturers, including General Motors, Ford, Honda and Daewoo, have set up plants in India, but there are also Indian companies. Hindustan Motors, with annual sales income of more than Rs 7.3 billion (US$165 million), is the oldest, and produced the first Indian car in 1942. The biggest company, Maruti Udyog Ltd (MUL), was established in 1981 as a joint enterprise between the Indian government and Suzuki of Japan.

ELECTRONICS

The electronics industry is expanding rapidly and now supplies almost all the computer disk drives, dot matrix printers, plotters, monitors and keyboards used in India. Computers, TV sets, microwave ovens and washing machines are also manufactured in India. In addition to domestic goods, the industry produces electronic components for communications.

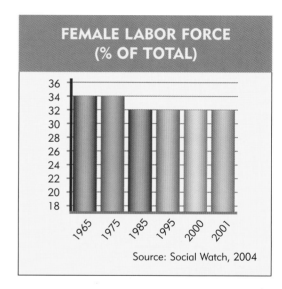

FEMALE LABOR FORCE (% OF TOTAL)

Source: Social Watch, 2004

The end of the production line at the Hindustan Motors plant at Thiruvallur, Tamil Nadu.

Workers assembling computer monitors at a factory near Bangalore, Karnataka.

manufacture hardware to established designs. There is no Indian company manufacturing semiconductors – the "chips" that lie at the heart of every electronic device; these must be imported.

Many of the Bangalore enterprises are engaged in supplying software services. When an organization needs a computer program to perform particular functions, a Bangalore company will be able to write and develop it. In years to come, the industry may begin to compete globally with entirely new electronic products.

Much of the electronics industry is centered in and around the city of Bangalore, Karnataka, India's fastest-growing city, with a population of more than 4 million. The city has a high concentration of electronics companies that

CALL CENTERS

Phone calls from customers needing advice about products or services, or help in using them, are usually directed to dedicated call centers. These now handle a very wide variety of inquires, and they also sell products by telephone – "telemarketing."

Call centers are major employers, which means their payroll expenses are high. In recent years, a growing number of Western companies have relocated their call centers to India, where wages are lower and operating costs are 40 percent cheaper. By March 2004, European and American companies had recruited 170,000 call center workers in India, and the number is expected to reach 1.1 million by 2008. Many Indian call centers are in Bangalore.

All Indian call center workers are university graduates who speak good English. They earn the equivalent of about $70 a week. A call center worker in the Unites States would be paid about $450 a week, but the Indian salary is about the same as that of a newly qualified doctor and twice a teacher's salary.

These workers at a call center in Bangalore, Karnataka, may well be talking to customers in the United States.

A plane at Bangalore airport belonging to Air Deccan, India's first budget airline.

RAIL

India has the second-largest rail network in the world, after China. More than 63,000km of track link 6,856 train stations, and every day Indian Railways (IR) runs about 8,700 passenger and 5,700 freight trains, carrying more than 1 million tonnes of freight and about 14 million passengers.

Indian Railways is a state-owned company that manages the entire network, together with the train stations and services such as cleaning and catering. The network is divided geographically into 16 zones. In addition, the Kolkata Metro, India's first underground service, is owned and operated by IR but is not included in any of the zones, and the Konkan Railway is a separate but incorporated operation. It runs for 760km along the Konkan Coast from Mumbai to Thiruvananthapuram in southern Kerala, across 2,137 bridges and 140 rivers, and through 83km of tunnel. It is the country's fastest service, traveling at 160km/h.

Of the total track, 45,000km is broad gauge, 14,800km meter gauge and 3,300km narrow gauge. In effect this means there are three separate networks. The company has begun to replace the meter- and narrow-gauge track so that the entire network will eventually consist of broad-gauge track. The plan is then to bring in faster trains, running at up to 160km/h.

ROAD, SEA AND AIR

Major cities are linked by 52,000km of well-maintained national highways. State highways cover 129,000km and there are also many minor roads, some no more than dirt tracks, which crisscross the country. Many people now travel by private car, but there is also an extensive bus network linking the cities and traveling into more remote regions.

Passenger ferries link some coastal cities, such as Kolkata and Chennai, and ocean liners

Passengers leaving a crowded commuter train at Mumbai station.

TRANSPORT

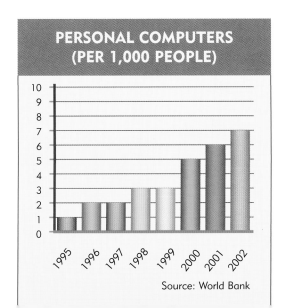

- Main road
- ┄┄┄┄ Railway
- ✈ International airport

0 — 500km
0 — 300 miles

operate passenger services to the Andaman and Lakshadweep Islands.

Air India provides air links between India and the outside world. Inside the country, Indian Airlines flies between seven international and more than 88 regional airports. Vayudoot is a domestic airline with plans to expand to reach more than 140 airports, serving the remotest parts of India.

TELEPHONES, TV, RADIO AND NEWSPAPERS

Telephone lines do not reach some of the remotest villages, but service is growing and most will be connected by about 2007. Private telephones are uncommon; most phones are for public use. Very few people have mobile phones (see table below), but these are gradually becoming more widespread.

More people have a TV than have a telephone, and the number is increasing with the spread of satellite and cable TV. There are about 83 TV sets for every 1,000 people. Radio reaches a much bigger audience. There are 120 radios for every 1,000 people.

Indian daily newspapers have a combined circulation of about 19 million. This is about a third the daily circulation in the United States, and is small for such a populous country. As well as the national dailies, there are many regional and local newspapers.

TELECOMMUNICATIONS DATA (PER 1,000 PEOPLE)

Mainline Phones	40
Mobile Phones	12
Internet Users	16

Source: World Bank

PERSONAL COMPUTERS (PER 1,000 PEOPLE)

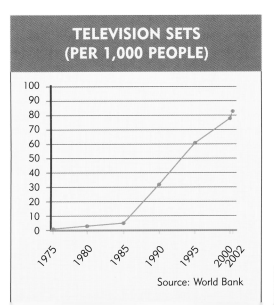

Source: World Bank

TELEVISION SETS (PER 1,000 PEOPLE)

Source: World Bank

A porter is enveloped in clouds of exhaust fumes and unable to move through a traffic jam in New Delhi.

THE ENVIRONMENT

India has more than 20 cities with more than 1 million inhabitants. New Delhi, Mumbai, Chennai and Kolkata are among the most polluted cities in the world, and more people die prematurely due to air pollution in India than in any other country.

A 1976 amendment to the Indian constitution committed the government to safeguarding the quality of the environment. This commitment was reinforced by the Environment Protection Act, passed in 1986.

In New Delhi it is illegal to drive any vehicle that is more than 15 years old, and in New Delhi, Mumbai, Chennai and Kolkata emission standards for private cars and commercial vehicles now match those in the European Union. Buses that run on compressed natural gas (CNG) are replacing New Delhi's diesel buses. CNG is a much cleaner fuel.

Half of the energy used in India comes from burning coal, which produces pollution. The government is encouraging the development of renewable energy resources. It favors solar energy, principally as a means of supplying electricity to small villages in remote rural areas. In these situations, solar cells are more economical than conventional sources of power. India also hopes to generate more power from large-scale hydroelectric systems.

Students cleaning the solar panels that heat water for their school in the Rishi Valley, Andhra Pradesh.

Bengal tigers resting by a stream in
Ranthambhore National Park, Rajasthan.

India contains 60 percent of the world's tigers, and until 1970 it was legal to hunt them for their skins. Hunters killed more than 3,000 tigers during the 1950s and early 1960s.

When people realized that the number of tigers was decreasing alarmingly, the authorities took action. Project Tiger was launched on 1 April 1973, in Corbett National Park in Uttar Pradesh. The Corbett National Park is still the most famous tiger reserve, but there are 66 protected areas for tigers. Despite the conservation efforts, however, there are now probably no more than about 3,000 tigers in the wild in India.

India has 65 national parks and more than 300 wildlife sanctuaries listed with the United Nations. Many of these are open to visitors and they are major tourist attractions.

AFFECTED ENVIRONMENTS

Soil degradation, due to erosion, overgrazing, waterlogging and salinization, is serious in some areas. Improved farming methods and more efficient irrigation are being encouraged as a way of restoring damaged soil and preventing further loss.

Water pollution is serious in some cities, where untreated sewage and industrial effluents contaminate rivers. Although increasing numbers of people have access to a piped water supply, 2 percent of the population obtain drinking water from a river or canal.

Wildlife is also threatened, particularly through loss of habitat – for example, where forests have been cut down to make way for farmland. India contains 172 animal species considered globally threatened by the International Union for Nature Conservation (IUCN) – 2.9 percent of the world's threatened species. These include Jenkin's shrew, the Namdapha flying squirrel, Salim Ali's fruit bat and Wroughton's free-tailed bat, all of which are found only in India. The Asian elephant, Indian rhinoceros and Ganges River dolphin are also threatened, as well as the Bengal tiger (see case study above).

The worst industrial accident the world has ever seen occurred on the night of 2–3 December 1984, at Bhopal, Madhya Pradesh, where a subsidiary of the US company Union Carbide was manufacturing pesticides.

The incident began when water accidentally flowed into a storage tank containing methyl isocyanate (MIC), triggering a reaction that released extremely poisonous MIC gas. At about 11:30 pm workers felt their eyes burning and told their supervisor, but the leak continued for two hours. MIC gas is heavier then air. It settled to the ground and flowed downwind for about 8km through a residential area where people were sleeping. At least 3,000 people were fatally poisoned and hundreds of thousands were injured. Many of the survivors were left with chronic illnesses affecting their eyes, muscles, respiratory system, digestion and nervous system.

LEISURE AND TOURISM

Baga Beach, Goa, offers a wide expanse of soft white sand.

As India grows more prosperous, increasing numbers of Indians can afford to take vacations. Many of them choose to travel abroad; in 2003, 4.5 million Indians did so, and that number is increasing. The United States is their most popular destination, but the tourist boards of many other countries are opening offices in India in an attempt to attract a share of this business. Indian visitors are popular because it is felt that many are more interested in food and shopping than in sightseeing, and so they tend to spend more than tourists from other countries.

Most Indians, however, prefer to take their vacations in their own country. In 2003, 300 million Indian citizens visited tourist areas. Surprisingly, perhaps, the majority of domestic tourists live in rural areas rather than the

CASE STUDY
BOLLYWOOD

India has a thriving movie industry, nicknamed "Bollywood," producing up to 1,000 feature films a year. Films featuring mythology, melodrama, romance, action and suspense, with songs and dances, are known as "Bombay talkies" or "masala movies" (masala is a mixture of spices). India is perhaps the only country in the world where home-produced movies attract much bigger audiences than imported US movies. The films are filled with popular heroes and heroines, song-and-dance routines, well-choreographed fights and simple story lines.

These people in Sikkim are waiting to buy tickets to see the latest Bollywood movie.

cities. Many are visiting relatives or friends and visit tourist attractions in the same area. These "social travelers" account for 59 percent of domestic tourists. Pilgrims and those visiting religious sites account for a further 14 percent. So many travelers are now Indian that the major hotels are offering attractive packages to domestic visitors.

FOREIGN VISITORS

Foreign vacationers have also discovered India, which is now rated one of the world's most popular tourist destinations. In 2003, India welcomed 2.8 million overseas visitors, from Europe, North America, Asia, Africa, Australia and New Zealand. About 30 percent of them were from the United Kingdom and the United States.

POPULAR ATTRACTIONS

It is now easier than ever before for tourists to explore India. The network of national highways provides well-maintained roads, and airfares have fallen. International airlines have increased the frequency of flights to India – although at peak times demand sometimes outstrips supply.

Kerala is the most popular tourist region for Indians. Situated between the Arabian Sea and the Western Ghats, the state has wide, palm-fringed beaches, boat trips along extensive waterways, and wildlife reserves. It is also famed for its version of Ayurvedic medical treatments, which use therapies based on herbal medicines.

Most foreign tourists visit the Taj Mahal, one of the most famous buildings in the world. It is in Agra, Uttar Pradesh, the former Mughal capital of India and only 204km from New Delhi, the modern capital.

Goa is a popular area with both Indian and Western tourists. It has buildings that reflect its past as a Portuguese colony, including whitewashed churches and grand cathedrals. There are also coconut plantations, rice fields and Hindu temples, as well as beaches stretching for more than 100km along the Konkan Coast.

The Taj Mahal at Agra, Uttar Pradesh, attracts large numbers of tourists.

Tourism is now a major industry in India. In 2003 its turnover was nearly Rs 400 million. Although India has captured only about 0.4 percent of the global tourism market, tourism already provides almost 20 million jobs, and after textiles and diamonds, it is the third-highest earner of foreign income. Economists predict that the industry will continue to expand rapidly.

LOOKING AHEAD

India is classed as a developing country, but it is changing rapidly. Already it is a major industrial nation, exporting manufactured goods to many parts of the world. Within the next few years Americans and Europeans may well be driving cars made in India and then, following the Japanese model, cars assembled locally in Indian-owned factories. India will also be exporting computers and other electronic devices, taking part of the market now held by other Asian countries.

Because of its size, however, Indian development is likely to be regional rather than being concentrated in a few areas. By 2050, India may be a leading economic power as well as the world's most populous nation, while retaining its vibrant cultural diversity.

Burst of monsoon The abrupt onset of the wet summer southwesterly monsoon, which begins with a violent rainstorm that ends the long drought.

Caste system A Hindu social structure that divides people into occupational groups. Individuals are born into a caste. Traditionally it was impossible for anyone to move from one caste to another and there was little informal social contact between members of different castes.

Cold War The rivalry between capitalist and socialist economic and political systems that emerged after World War II and developed into a military standoff between members of the North Atlantic Treaty Organization (NATO) and of the Soviet-led Warsaw Pact. It ended with the political collapse of the Soviet Union.

Dalit The people formerly classed as "untouchable" in the Hindu caste system. Dalit, their own name for themselves, means "depressed."

Desert Any region where the annual rainfall is less than the amount of water that could evaporate during the same period. The amount of rainfall below which deserts form varies according to the average temperature, but less than 25mm of rain a year will produce desert almost anywhere.

Floodplain Level land on either side of a river that is periodically inundated when the river overflows its banks or that is immersed as meanders in the river advance across the area.

GDP (Gross Domestic Product) A measure of national income. The value of all the goods and services produced within a country over a stated period (usually one year), charged at market prices and including taxes and subsidies (treated as negative taxes).

Ghats Literally, "steps." The Western and Eastern Ghats are ranges of mountains that run some distance inland and parallel to the western and eastern coasts of India, respectively.

GNI (Gross National Income) The monetary value of goods and services produced by a country plus any earnings from overseas in a single year. It used to be called Gross National Product (GNP).

Green revolution A program of agricultural reform and modernization, based on the introduction of new varieties of wheat and rice and the technologies to grow them, that was devised and coordinated by the Food and Agriculture Organization (FAO) of the UN in the 1960s.

Humidity The amount of water vapor (not liquid droplets or ice crystals such as cloud or fog) present in the air.

ITCZ (intertropical convergence zone) A belt around the Earth where the trade winds from the Northern and Southern Hemispheres meet.

Jet stream A ribbon of wind blowing at 105–500km/h at an altitude of 7.5–12km.

Lok Sabha The House of the People; the lower house of the Indian parliament.

Mangrove A tree that grows in coastal mud below the high-tide line. There are many species. Mangroves trap mud and thereby extend the coastline.

Monsoon A season of extreme weather characterized by the direction of the prevailing wind. India has a monsoon climate comprising a dry, northeasterly winter monsoon and a wet, southwesterly summer monsoon.

Paddy A field of rice that is flooded for part of the growing season, or rice grown in such a field.

Pangaea A supercontinent that came into being about 240 million years ago, when all the world's continents united. Pangaea lasted for about 40 million years before starting to break up.

Pastoralist A person who earns a living by herding livestock, driving them from one area of seasonal pasture to another. Pastoralists are either nomads or have permanent homes but spend part of each year away from home, tending their animals.

Plebiscite A referendum, or vote of all the people on a single issue.

Princely states More than 560 regions of the Indian subcontinent that were outside direct British control prior to independence. Each had its own ruler, but the ruling princes had to remain on good terms with the British. After independence the princely states were incorporated into either India or Pakistan.

Rajya Sabha The Council of State; the upper house of the Indian parliament.

Salinization The accumulation of mineral salts near the soil surface, usually linked to waterlogging and caused by poor irrigation. Salinization can render the soil sterile.

Snow line The elevation on a mountainside above which snow lies throughout the year.

Supercontinent A continent formed by the union of smaller continents.

Total fertility rate (TFR) The average number of surviving babies born to each woman in the course of her life. A population with a TFR of 2.1 will remain the same size. A TFR higher than 2.1 means the population will increase, and a TFR of less than 2.1 means the population will decrease in size.

Trade wind The wind that blows in the Tropics, from the northeast in the Northern Hemisphere and from the southeast in the Southern Hemisphere. Trade winds blow reliably along the same track; "trade" is an old word for "track."

Tribal people Members of communities that did not accept the caste system at the time when Hinduism was established. They live in the more remote forest and mountain regions away from the mainstream of society.

Tube well A well made by driving a tube vertically downward into the ground until it lies below the water table and the lower part fills with water. Also called a driven well.

Waterlogging The accumulation of water below ground.

FURTHER INFORMATION

BOOKS TO READ:

Abram, David, Devdan Sen, Nicki Edwards, Mike Ford, and Beth Wooldridge. *The Rough Guide to India.* 5th ed. London: Rough Guides, 2003. A detailed guide with much historical information

Lambda, Abha Narain. *Eyewitness Travel Guides: India.* New York: Dorling Kindersley, 2002. A highly illustrated guide to all parts of India, with many geographical and historical details.

Sekhon, Joti. *Modern India.* Boston: McGraw-Hill, 2000. A good short description of India, its history, religions, society and politics.

Tammita-Delgoda, SinhaRaja. *A Traveller's History of India.* 2d ed. Brooklyn, N.Y.: Interlink Books, 1999. A brief, highly readable history of India.

WEBSITES:

Ancient India: The Land and Its Peoples
http://www.wsu.edu/~dee/ANCINDIA/LAND.HTM

Gateway to Districts of India on the Web
http://districts.nic.in/

India Community Forestry Profile
www.forestsandcommunities.org/Country_Profiles/india.html

India – Geography
http://countrystudies.us/india/27.htm

India Image: A Gateway to Government of India
http://indiaimage.nic.in/

India – Tribes
http://countrystudies.us/india/70.htm

Population of India
http://www.indianchild.com/population_of_india.htm

CIA World Factbook
http://www.cia.gov/cia/publications/factbook/geos/in.html

METRIC CONVERSION TABLE

To convert	to	do this
mm (millimeters)	inches	divide by 25.4
cm (centimeters)	inches	divide by 2.54
m (meters)	feet	multiply by 3.281
m (meters)	yards	multiply by 1.094
km (kilometers)	yards	multiply by 1094
km (kilometers)	miles	divide by 1.6093
kilometers per hour	miles per hour	divide by 1.6093
cm^2 (square centimeters)	square inches	divide by 6.452
m^2 (square meters)	square feet	multiply by 10.76
m^2 (square meters)	square yards	multiply by 1.196
km^2 (square kilometers)	square miles	divide by 2.59
km^2 (square kilometers)	acres	multiply by 247.1
hectares	acres	multiply by 2.471
cm^3 (cubic centimeters)	cubic inches	multiply by 16.387
m^3 (cubic meters)	cubic yards	multiply by 1.308
l (liters)	pints	multiply by 2.113
l (liters)	gallons	divide by 3.785
g (grams)	ounces	divide by 28.329
kg (kilograms)	pounds	multiply by 2.205
metric tonnes	short tons	multiply by 1.1023
metric tonnes	long tons	multiply by 0.9842
BTUs (British thermal units)	kWh (kilowatt-hours)	divide by 3,415.3
watts	horsepower	multiply by 0.001341
kWh (kilowatt-hours)	horsepower-hours	multiply by 1.341
MW (megawatts)	horsepower	multiply by 1,341
gigawatts per hour	horsepower per hour	multiply by 1,341,000
°C (degrees Celsius)	°F (degrees Fahrenheit)	multiply by 1.8 then add 32

Numbers shown in **bold** refer to pages with maps, graphic illustrations or photographs.

Domesticated working elephants walk through a river at Satpura, Madhya Pradesh.